A Rambler's Guide to
CORRIB COUNTRY

Natural Environment • Archaeology • History • Navigation Channel

Hen's Castle or Caisleán na Circe (99E-50N)

A Naturalist's Lake.

The most impressive aspect of Loch Corrib is it's scale. The shoreline of fen, limestone grassland, marsh, bog and wood is well over 200 km in length and many rare and beautiful plants grow there. There are over a hundred islands, most are unfarmed and unoccupied and even yet only a minority have been surveyed by naturalists. Huge numbers of birds winter on the lake. The extent of open water is so great as to remind one of the sea.

Life in the Water

The very water itself contains a wealth of planktonic organisms but these are too small to be seen without magnification. An exception is the occasional growth of algal scums which are all too visible and caused by unwanted and dangerous fertiliser pollution. Amongst the varied animal plankton is the shrimp *Mysis relicta*, a species surviving from the immediate post glacial period. Most submerged limestone rocks are covered by a yellow brown gritty crust, which is easily detached by hand. This crust is composed of a variety of primitive blue-green algae. It covers a huge area of rock and may play an important ecological role, but as yet it has been little studied. It is often associated with the pit and pinnacle weathering of shore side limestone and may be a possible cause of this strange erosion. The most striking evidence of planktonic life is seen not in the lake itself but in the small lakeside rock pools; here occasional pools have turned bright red due to the growth of an alga. Mussels are of course, salt water animals, but a related shellfish - the Swan mussel (*Anodonta*)- can be seen in soft mud. The more valuable Pearl Mussel (*Unio*) also occurs in rivers flowing into the northwest arm of the lake. Water snails while difficult to identify by the amateur, occur in great abundance and drifts of empty shells are frequent. The Freshwater Crayfish (*Astacus pallipes*) is known from tributaries of the lake. Equally, insect life is the realm of the specialist but even the passer-by will notice the colourful dragonflies and huge clouds of midges and caddis-flies along rocky shores. In sheltered places, Water Boatmen, Water Stick insects and Whirligig beetles swim and dive and even walk across the water. At greater depths many types of insect larvae play an important part in the lake's food chain, which supports a well developed Brown Trout fishery.

Fish

Fish fascinate both naturalists and anglers. Native species include the Brown Trout, the Salmon, the Char and the Eel; the status of the Pike (*Esox lucius*) and Perch is debatable while the Rudd (*Scardinius erythrophthalmus*), Bream (*Abramis brama*) and Roach (*Rutilus rutilus*) are definitely introduced. A deep water variety of Trout, the ferox trout is strikingly large and fish can exceed 10 kg in weight. The Arctic Char is like the shrimp *Mysis relicta*, a survivor from colder times. The hatching of the Mayfly on the Corrib draws anglers from all over Ireland. During the month of May, boats with long dapping rods extended can be seen drifting across the lake. Throughout the year, fishermen are the most frequent travellers on the water.

Flowers of the Lakeside

The plant life of Loch Corrib may at first seem sparse as few plants grow in the shallow water off rocky shores. However such a view is deceptive; the shores, islands and environs of the lake contain a huge variety of species. Water plants include the scarce *Potomageton filiformis* and other species. Stoneworts (*Chara sp.*) cover much of the lower lake while Marsh Pennywort (*Hydrocotyle vulgaris*) and *Littorella uniflora* occur below the winter flood line. Everywhere amongst the waterside rocks, Water Mint (*Mentha aquatica*), Wild Angelica (*Angelica sylvestris*), Hemp Agrimony (*Eupatorium cannabinum*), Purple Loosestrife, and Bog Pimpernel (*Anagallis tenella*) are to be found. Lakeside fens and marshes are full of Meadowsweet, (*Filipendula ulmaria*) Northern Bedstraw, Black Bog Rush, Butterwort (*Pinguicula vulgaris*). Drier ground supports a colourful limestone grassland of Blue Moor Grass (*Sesleria albicans*), Columbine (*Aquilegia vulgaris*), Thyme (*Thymus praecox*), Catsfoot (*Antennaria dioica*), Bird's Foot, Lady's Bedstraw (*Galium verum*), Harebell (*Campanula rotundifolia*) and many others. A great variety of Orchids are to be seen including the Early Purple, the Marsh Helleborine, the Frog Orchid (*Coeloglossum viride*), the Butterfly Orchid (*Platanthera sp.*), the Pyramidal (*Anacamptis pyramidalis*) and Fragrant Orchids (*Gymnadenia conopsea*) as well as several much rarer species.

VEGETATION OF THE SHORES AND ISLANDS

Farmland adjoins much of the mainland shore while many islands are neither grazed or farmed today. This difference in land use is reflected in very different vegetation. In limestone areas, Hazel scrub, grassland or improved pasture are the major types. In many places a flora all but identical to that of the Burren occurs and Gentians, Juniper (*Juniperus communis*) and Bloody Cranesbill (*Geranium sanguineum*) are common in certain places such as Luimnagh (28E-41N). Hazel scrub contains many typical woodland plants such as Wood Anemone, Bluebells, Primrose and Wood Sanicle (*Sanicula europaea*). Farmland is less distinctive but in the hedgerow trees and shrubs such as Whitethorn (*Crataegus monogyna*), Ash (*Fraxinus excelsior*), Whitebeam (*Sorbus aria*), Spindle (*Euonymus europaeus*) and Willow (*Salix sp*) are often seen. In the northwest, a flora more typical of poorer land appears, with areas of blanket bog, heath and grassland. Plants which avoid lime predominate, with hedges of Fuchsia, Pennywort (*Umbilicus rupestris*) and English Stonecrop (*Sedum anglicum*) on rocks and walls, Bog Asphodel (*Narthecium ossifragum*) and Sundew (*Drosera sp.*) on wet ground, Heather and Sheepsbit (*Jasione montana*) in drier places. The island flora is of interest as it is undisturbed and in many places a transition from lakeshore to woodland can be seen. Ash, Buckthorn (*Rhamnus cathartica*), Guelder Rose (*Viburnum opulus*), Birch (*Betula*) and Alder (*Alnus glutinosa*) grow everywhere while self sown Scots Pine (*Pinus sylvestris*) occur on many islands.

WOODS

While much of the woodland around the Corrib only developed since 1850, certain island and mainland woods may well be very old. A 16th century map of Ireland, suggests that woods persisted on much of the west and north east of Loch Corrib during that century, while the more fertile eastern side appeared largely cleared. In the nineteenth century a list of native woodlands on the mainland had shrunk to include only small fragments at Doon (02E-49N), Annagh (18E-36N), Glann, (11E-46N) Gortdarragh (18E-40N), Kilbeg (23E-42N) and Kilroe (31E-41N). By the twentieth century large trees only occurred at Doon and a few places on the Glann shore. However Hazel scrub persists at several of these locations and the list of old woodland indicator species

Church and Fortified House East of Cross Village (20E-55N)

Detail of Doorway in Teampall na Naomh, Inchagoill (12E-49N)

Kilcronan Children's Burial Ground (21E-44N)

Standing Stones beside Moyne Church (5E-50N)

Ross Friary (24E-48N)

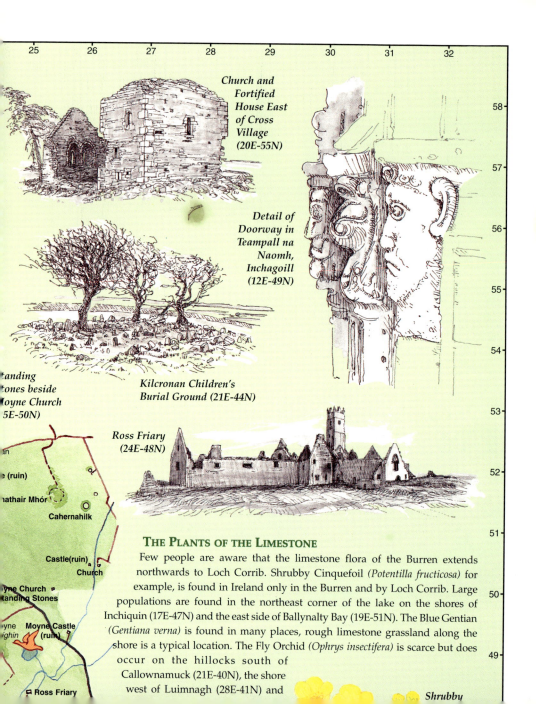

THE PLANTS OF THE LIMESTONE

Few people are aware that the limestone flora of the Burren extends northwards to Loch Corrib. Shrubby Cinquefoil (*Potentilla fructicosa*) for example, is found in Ireland only in the Burren and by Loch Corrib. Large populations are found in the northeast corner of the lake on the shores of Inchiquin (17E-47N) and the east side of Ballynalty Bay (19E-51N). The Blue Gentian (*Gentiana verna*) is found in many places, rough limestone grassland along the shore is a typical location. The Fly Orchid (*Ophrys insectifera*) is scarce but does occur on the hillocks south of Callownamuck (21E-40N), the shore west of Luimnagh (28E-41N) and

Shrubby

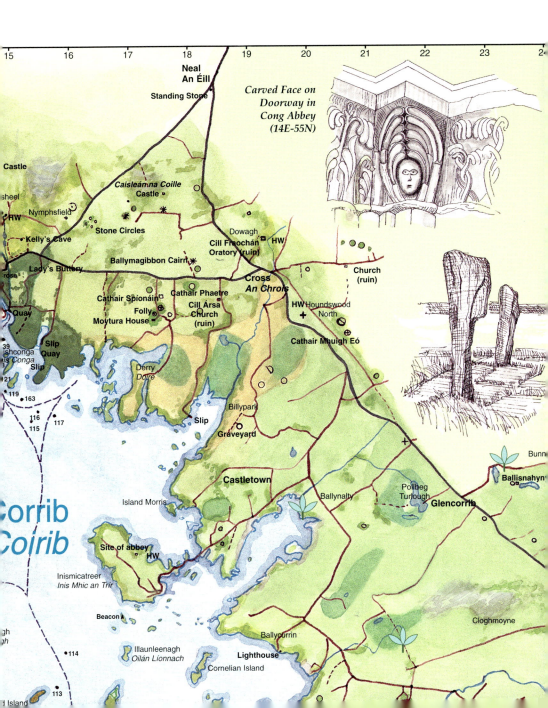

fort which was built perhaps 2,000 years ago. Today it is half concealed in Hazel scrub but a visitor is still rewarded by the surprising view of the fertile plain, the great lake and distant mountains that is to be seen from the hill top.

The commonest ancient monument in Ireland is the ring fort also known as a rath, lios, caiseal or dún. These structures were much smaller than Cathair Mór and their name, ringfort, is perhaps a slight misnomer as these circular earthen or stone banks probably mark the site of ancient farmsteads more than military positions. Very few forts were built on the ancient quartzites of the north and west, while the light limestone soils between Headford and Cong support a density of over one ringfort per square kilometre. Many are partially demolished or heavily overgrown by bushes. To the west of the lake, the small area of limestone has some dúns but their traces almost vanish once one crosses onto the ancient granites of Iar Connacht.

It is now thought that the great majority of forts were constructed in the early Christian period (AD 400-1200). The earliest written records commence in this period. We are told that around AD 600 the Limestone plain east of the Corrib was the territory of the Uí Briúin Seola with the Con Maicne Tire in present day South Mayo. While most ringforts were essentially farmsteads, several were of military value. Hidden amongst the trees of Inish Cairbre (22E-43N) in Cairgin Bay is a magnificent stone fort or caiseal surrounded by a deep moat. In the Norman Invasion of 1236, it was of strategic importance in the control of the lake's shipping. Other well preserved stone forts include Cahergal (26E-45N) and Cathair Mayo (20E-54N). An underground room or souterrain is a feature of many forts, but most of these are now blocked or have collapsed.

Ancient Oratory Known as Teampall Beag na Naomh(18E-37N)

THE CELTIC CHURCH

The coming of Christianity was marked by many changes in early Irish society. Hidden away on islands or copses or even in patches of scrub, the mostly neglected remnants of early Christian oratories still survive. At Dowagh (19E-55N), or amidst brambles in a field east of Rosscahill (18E-37N) the walls and gables of these simple buildings survive as a reminder of the Celtic Church. The names of the men who founded these churches are still venerated. St Fursey, St Cuanna and St Annin are examples of early saints who lived around the lake. In many places prayers are still said at Holy Wells dedicated to saints, although it is also believed that some of these wells were sacred even before the coming of Christianity. At sites such as Moyne Church (25E-50N) the ancient monastic boundaries still remain, along with two standing stones between which by tradition, coffins were passed before burial.

Archaeological excavations at Moyne revealed numerous fragments of red deer bones, a forest animal which in turn suggests the presence of extensive woods even at that time.

Bullaun Stone at Moyne Church (25E-50N)

Romanesque Doorway of Teampall na Naomh, Inchagoill (12E-49N)

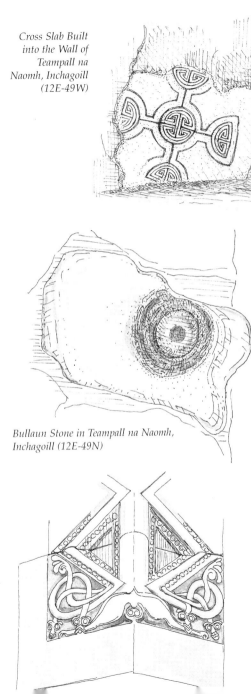

Cross Slab Built into the Wall of Teampall na Naomh, Inchagoill (12E-49W)

Bullaun Stone in Teampall na Naomh, Inchagoill (12E-49N)

The most impressive and best conserved early churches are on Inchagoill (12E-49N), an island which is easily reached by ferry from Oughterard or Cong. One of the earliest inscriptions in Latin letters known from Ireland, is found on an erect stone on the island, while nearby, a magnificent romanesque doorway contrasts with the earlier simplicity of a neighbouring church. (The unfortunate pocking of the carved stone in the doorway is due to the type of sandstone used). Monasteries were also founded on Inishmicatrir and Inchiquin but very few traces remain. At Kilcoona (31E-44N) the foundations of a round tower and church remain. Church life flourished through out the middle ages and remnants of once great monasteries are to be seen at Annaghdown (28E-37N) and Cong; the quality of the stone carvings is a reminder of the former prosperity of the region in the 12th century.

Detail of Window in Annaghdown Cathedral (28E-38N)

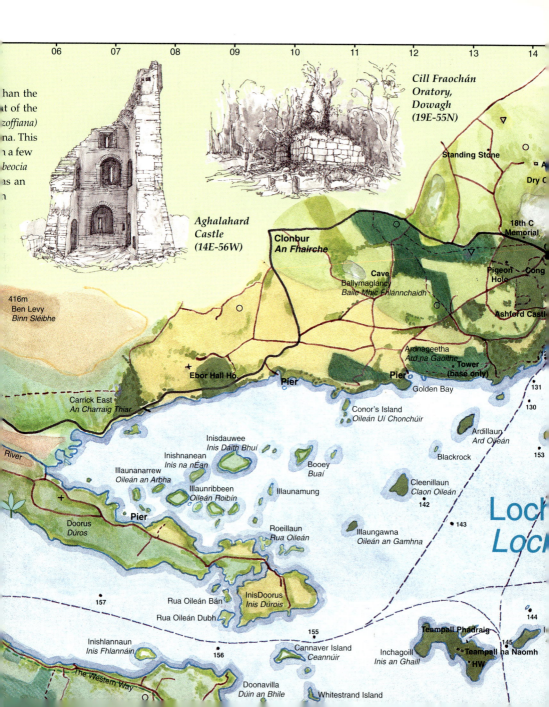

PLANTS OF THE SLATES AND SCHISTS

The rocks on the north west shores of the Corrib are [not]
limestones and lime poor. Perhaps the most interesti[ng ...of the]
entire lake is the Irish Lady's Tresses Orchid (*Spiranthes [romanzoffiana*])
which grows on the shore between Oughterard and Co[ng. This]
pretty orchid is a North American plant which is also fo[und in a few]
places in Ireland and Britain. The St Dabeoc's Hea[th (*Daboecia*]
cantabrica) which grows on rocks and dry heathy gro[und has an]
even more restricted distribution, occurring only in w[estern]
Connacht, and the Atlantic regions of France, Spai[n and]
Portugal. St Patrick's Cabbage (*Saxifraga spathularis*) s[hares]
the same general distribution as the St Dabeoc's heath [and is]
found on rocks and in some Oak woods. It's delicate sp[rays of]
white flowers appear in early summer, although th[e]
tough leathery leaves carpet
rock outcrops all year.

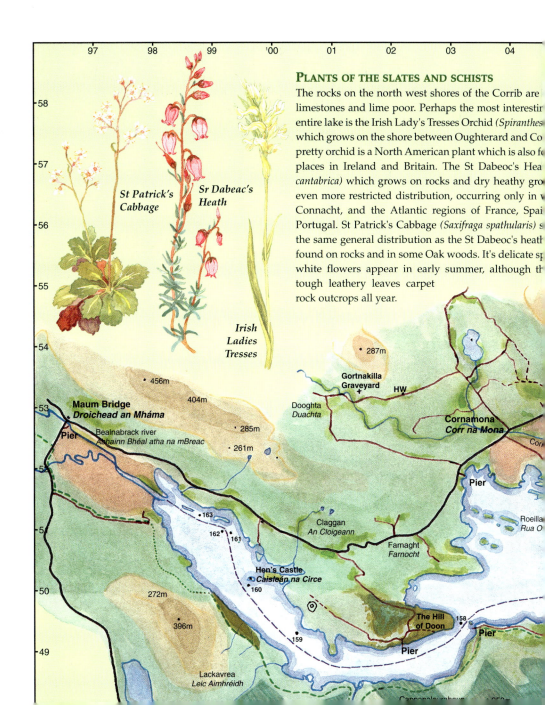

sailing boats were in use for carrying goods and passengers. A series of quays were constructed and after mid century a regular steamer service operated. Stone, turf, crops and livestock were carried as well as a constant traffic of people going to market or visiting. The poet Antony Raftery's best known work – *Eanach Dhúin* – describes the disaster off Menlough in which 19 people were drowned on the way to market in Galway in 1828.

Trade was extensive. Many of the lakeside bogs were cut for fuel. Ore was occasionally shipped from the Glann mines (05E-48N). What may be a remnant of an old brick works can be seen at Woodpark (29E-36N), the bricks appear to have been made from lake mud and fired with peat. Wood Quay in Galway city was the terminus for this lake borne trade, which as Raftery relates, also included sheep and cattle. Imported goods, such as seaweed from Connemara and porter were carried up the lake from Galway.

Lighthouse at Ballycurrin (19E-49N)

AFTER THE FAMINE

The coming of the Famine in 1845 was the start of a series of great changes which together have produced the Loch Corrib we see today. The human population eventually fell to half it's 19th century maximum and deserted farms and cottages can still be seen on marginal or mountain land. A little of the misery of those times can still be felt in the Cillíns or Children's burial grounds that are so frequent around the lake. These were mostly used to inter unbaptised children but in many cases famine victims were also laid to rest there. The old landlords, especially the Martin family went bankrupt and most of the large demesnes had fallen into their present state of ruin by the early 20th century. An exception was Ashford Castle at Cong which was bought and enlarged by the Guinness family in the late nineteenth century and is now a hotel. The collapse of the landlord system was brought about by tenant farmers' agitation and resulted in them gaining freehold possession of their land. Unfortunately this social revolution was matched by a decline in spoken Irish and the language is now only spoken in the districts around Menlough and Cornamona.

MODERNISATION AND LANDSCAPE CHANGE

These social and political reforms gave rise both to increased agricultural production and great changes in the region's ecology. The first great ecological change took place long before 1900. This was the Corrib drainage scheme of 1846-50. The winter lake level was lowered by 1 metre and many new islands were created from former reefs and banks. The previous shoreline is easily recognised both by water eroded stones and

Old Irish Inscription on Engraved Stone which Reads "The Stone of Luguaedon, son of Menb" Inchagoill (12E-49N)

Cill Cuimín Church (13E-42N)

FISH

All our native fish species colonized Ireland from the European mainland since the Ice Age. The only fish which managed to establish themselves were those which could live in and travel through fresh and salt water. Salmon (*Salmo salar*), trout (*Salmo trutta*) and eels (*Anguilla anguilla*) are the most important species. A very early arrival was the Arctic Char (*Salvelinus fontinalis*), a trout like fish which lives in the far north of Europe. As the climate warmed, populations of this fish became isolated in deep cold lakes. A small population still exists in the Corrib. The Trout is an extremely adaptable fish which occurs in small streams and lochans as well as in the large western lakes. The rich feeding of the Corrib regularly produces fish exceeding 2 kg. In addition, there is a population of very large Trout, sometimes called 'Ferox' trout which are much larger sometimes greater than 8 kg. The Perch (*Perca fluviatilis*) is probably an early introduction, as it is difficult to see how it might have reached the Corrib unaided. It is now a very common fish in the lake, but is considered by most anglers as a distraction from the main business of trout fishing.

small cliffs which are now several metres inland. In addition the Clare, Black (19E-47N) and Cregg (29E-34N) rivers were deepened and canalized. At Moyne a previously underground river was diverted into a canal which cuts through a limestone hill. An unfinished canal was cut between Loch Mask and the Corrib at Cong; to this day the canal is periodically dry as drainage still runs underground. Navigation was also improved and the present system of markers date from this time. Transport by water however all but ceased by the early twentieth century. Further drainage in this century destroyed several important turloughs east of the Corrib, while turf cutting removed several smaller bogs. Next to drainage the conversion of Hazel scrub and stoney ground to pasture by mechanical diggers has had the greatest visual impact on the landscape. The saddest case of this practice is the clearance of limestone pavement at Cloghmoyne (29E-42N) where the only Irish site of Limestone Fern (*Gymnocarpium robertianum*) is now almost destroyed. This trend has been accelerated by the division of commonage which has resulted in several areas of rough grazing or scrub being cleared and fenced.

An ever more dangerous threat is the widespread over-use of agricultural fertilizers on thin limestone soils; inevitably these fertilizers have penetrated into the ground water and then flowed into the lake. This enrichment is a huge danger to the aquatic ecosystem. Excess phosphate and nitrate will allow algal scums to proliferate and destroy much of the lake's aquatic life.

These pressures are part of a greater change within the communities that dwell around the lake. Bungalows are replacing more picturesque but less fashionable cottages. This change is not universal; in many parts of the Corrib country, especially the eastern side, neatly maintained thatched houses are interspersed amongst the now common bungalows. The towns of Cong, Headford, Moycullen and Oughterard are well kept and prosperous. While the population of towns and villages grows, the gradual withdrawal of people from marginal agricultural areas and indeed from the lake itself, continues. Most islands are now reverting to wood and scrub. On the mainland, Hazel is spreading in areas of former rough grazing and on limestone pavement.

The future of the lake will depend on how the nearby city of Galway expands, the direction tourism will take and our capacity to develop an agriculture which absorbs it's own wastes. What is certain is that so large a body of clear freshwater is more spectacular treasure than mere resource; it's future well being is totally entwined in the well being of those who live along it's shores.

EXPLORING THE LAKE.

The best way to explore Loch Corrib is by water. For those who prefer to let others worry about navigation, a regular ferry in summer crosses from Oughterard pier to Inchagoill and then to Cong. This trip takes in much of the upper lake and includes a long stopover on Inchagoill. A tour boat also operates from Galway and this long trip up the lake is well worth while.

For those who are more adventurous, boats with outboard motors can be hired. These will comfortably hold 4-5 people and can be obtained at many places around the lake. Further enquiries can be made in local shops or guesthouses. Obviously only those with boating experience should venture out by themselves. For fishermen the Western Regional Fishery board at Galway (Weir Lodge, Earl's Island Galway) will help with queries, while all the lakeside towns cater for anglers.

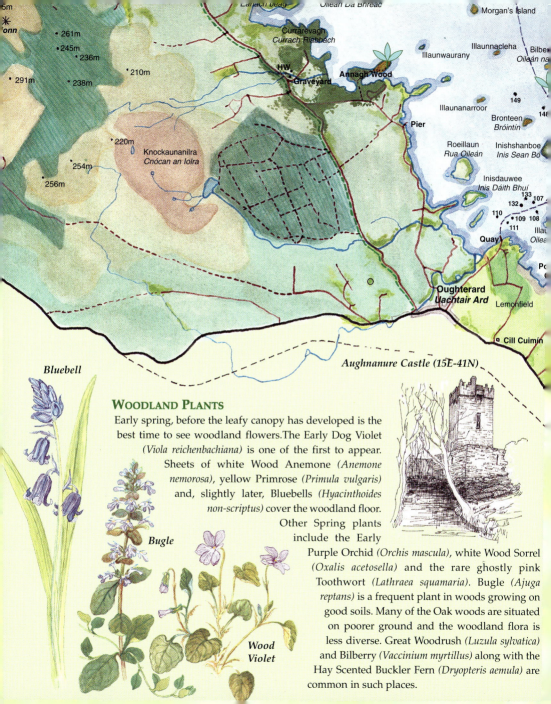

WOODLAND PLANTS

Early spring, before the leafy canopy has developed is the best time to see woodland flowers. The Early Dog Violet (*Viola reichenbachiana*) is one of the first to appear. Sheets of white Wood Anemone (*Anemone nemorosa*), yellow Primrose (*Primula vulgaris*) and, slightly later, Bluebells (*Hyacinthoides non-scriptus*) cover the woodland floor. Other Spring plants include the Early Purple Orchid (*Orchis mascula*), white Wood Sorrel (*Oxalis acetosella*) and the rare ghostly pink Toothwort (*Lathraea squamaria*). Bugle (*Ajuga reptans*) is a frequent plant in woods growing on good soils. Many of the Oak woods are situated on poorer ground and the woodland flora is less diverse. Great Woodrush (*Luzula sylvatica*) and Bilberry (*Vaccinium myrtillus*) along with the Hay Scented Buckler Fern (*Dryopteris aemula*) are common in such places.

foundations collapsed due to river erosion. The castle of Aghalahard (14E-56N) was the residence of the MacDonalds, galloglasses (professional soldiers) of the Burkes. This castle is unusually well built of cut limestone blocks. Many other castles were owned by local lords and were the fore runners of the later big houses of the 18th and 19th centuries.

Ross Friary (24E-48N), near Headford is one of the best preserved mediaeval monastic sites in the country. It was built sometime in the late 15th century for the Franciscan order. Despite the Reformation the friary was only finally abandoned in 1753. Although the friars had been expelled on many previous occasions, they managed to return, thanks to the support of local landowners. The ruins lack only a roof and still include a fish pond and the remains of a mill. Many old families are buried in the friary and funerary monuments include a magnificent 17th century coat of arms of the McDonalds in one of the side chapels.

Monk's Fishing House, Cong (14E-55N)

Ruined Church North of Headford (26E-50N)

O'FLAHERTIES AND BURKES

The Norman invasion of Ireland occurred at a time when the Kings of Connacht, the O'Connors were in conflict with the descendants of the Uí Briúin Seola, the O Flaherties. The lasting result of the invasion was that the Norman de Burgos forced the O'Flaherties to cede their territory east of Loch Corrib and to retreat west of the lake. There, the O'Flaherties gradually came to dominate all of Connemara during the middle ages. During this period another Norman family, the Joyces, established themselves in the country around the north west of Loch Corrib which to this day is known as Joyce's Country. This ancient political upheaval is still mirrored in the names of many of the present inhabitants. Joyce, Burke and O'Flaherty are amongst the commoner surnames seen on shops and businesses.

The Burkes and their allies brought many new customs with them, including the construction of stone castles. In the 13th century the Corrib was a frontier between Gaelic and Norman Ireland; the newly acquired good land between Kilbeg and Inchiquin, so vulnerable to raids across the narrow lake was defended by Castles at Cairgin (23E-43N) and Annaghkeen. These structures are noticeably different from the later and much commoner tower houses of the 15th and 16th centuries. The masonry is cruder and the plan is distinctive with an entrance on the first floor and a projecting tower used as a latrine. The Castle at Ballisnahyny may also be of this type. However the most impressive castle of this plan, Hen's Castle, was built by the kings of Connacht, the O'Connors, on Oileán na Circe in the north of the lake.

Within a century the De Burgoes renounced their allegiance to England and adopted Gaelic language, law and customs. The growing prosperity of Galway - then an Anglo Norman trading town - influenced the economy of the Corrib basin, as the lake itself was the main highway from the town into the interior of Connacht. Many churches, abbeys and tower houses were built at this time. Early improvements to navigation on the lake were the work of mediaeval monks. Many buildings of this period still remain around the lake, some even are still in use. The great castle, banqueting hall and bawn of Aughnanure (15E-41N), was the centre of power of the O'Flaherty family who by the date of building were lords of all Connemara. Unfortunately much of the splendid banqueting hall was lost when the

Detail of Window in Banqueting Hall, Aughnanure Castle (15E-41N)

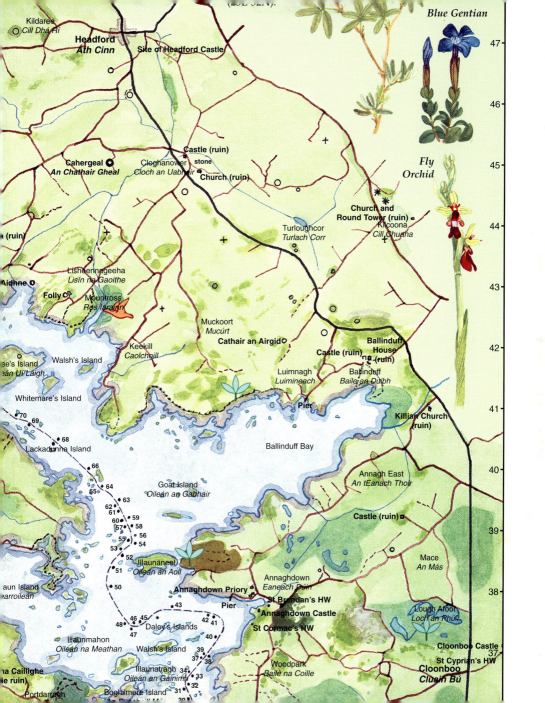

encountered in summer include the Heron (*Ardea cinerea*), the Merganser, the Great Crested Grebe and the Mute Swan (*Cygnus olor*). A variety of ducks breed, such as the Mallard (*Anas platyrhynchos*), the Tufted duck and the rare and recently arrived Common Scoter. The Lapwing (*Vanellus vanellus*), the Common Sandpiper *(Actitus hypoleucos)*, the Redshank *(Tringa totanus)* and the Ringed Plover (*Charadrius hiaticula*) nest amongst the lonelier rocky shores. The huge shallow expanse of the southern basin, with it's vast acreage of submerged water plants, is ideal habitat for wintering wild fowl. Populations of up to 20,000 pochard and 16,000 Coot have been recorded as well as smaller numbers of Whooper (*Cygnus cygnus*) and Bewick's Swan (*Cygnus columbianus*), Shoveler (*Anas clypeata*), Gadwall (*Anas strepera*) and Wigeon (*Anas penelope*). As the lake level rises in winter, shoreside pastures flood and waders, especially Golden Plover, (*Pluvialis apricaria*), Curlew (*Numenius arquata*), Redshank and Lapwing occur at many places. The magnificent Greenland Whitefronted Goose may also be seen, either high overhead or grazing on the larger islands or mainland shores. In winter moving about the lake is more difficult as most boats are taken out of the water and winter storms are frequent. Nevertheless much can be seen from the shore; especially on the callows and bogs that surround the Clare and Cregg rivers. The small wetlands at Moyne (24E-48N) and Ballisnahyny (23E-51N) also have a rich birdlife in winter.

There are many woodland and pasture birds and in recent years birds of conifer forest such as the Siskin (*Carduelis spinus*) and Crossbill (*Loxia curvirostra*) have established small populations in the large plantations west of the Corrib. Equally the Hen Harrier (*Circus cyaneus*) is increasing in frequency but birds of prey are limited in variety; the Kestrel (*Falco tinnunculus*), the Sparrow Hawk (*Accipiter nisus*) and the Peregrine (*Falco peregrinus*) nest and are most likely to be seen. Place names such as Cnocán an Iolra (07E-45N), "the small hill of the Eagle" suggest a greater diversity in the past.

MAMMALS

On warm calm evenings in summer there is an abundant insect life over the lake and Swallows (*Hirundo rustica*) and Martins (*Riparia riparia*) can be seen darting over the water. As dusk falls, one notices that birds are replaced by bats especially Daubenton's Bat (*Leuconoe daubentonii*) which is not uncommon. Most of Ireland's bats have been recorded around the Corrib, and the local Lesser Horseshoe Bat (*Rhinolophus hipposideros*) roosts in limestone caves, around Cong. Other mammals are less conspicuous but Badgers (*Meles meles*), Pine Martens (*Martes martes*), Stoat (*Mustela erminea*) are common. The Otter (*Lutra lutra*) is an important member of the lake's fauna, it's droppings or spraints and resting place or holt are often seen on the smaller islands. The introduced Mink (*Mustela vison*) is also found. On still nights the strange drawn out cry of the Vixen (*Vulpes vulpes*) can be heard, sometimes from far off across the lake. Feral Goats (*Capra hircus*) are met with occasionally, and Hedgehogs (*Erinaceus europaeus*), Hares (*Lepus timidus*) and Foxes are all to be seen, even during the day, in the many secluded copses and abandoned fields that surround the lake.

STONE AGE REMNANTS

The first human beings to see Loch Corrib were probably hunter gatherers of the middle stone or Mesolithic age perhaps 6,000 years ago. To

Loch Corrib, it's origin and size

Ireland is a country of many landscapes, but all belong either to the flat plains and wide bog land of the centre or the mountains and sea cliffs of the periphery. This division reflects the island's geology; a flat limestone core separated from the sea by harder, more contorted and generally older rocks. Like all boundaries in nature, the border between the central plain and the western mountains is interesting ground.

For reasons not yet fully understood, a series of large lakes has formed at many locations where limestone and less soluble rocks meet. Loch Leane beside Killarney straddles the boundary between sandstone and limestone, Loch Mask in Mayo divides the sandstone plateau of Maumtrasna from the limestone plain to the east, while Loch Conn, also in Mayo, has one shore of quartzite and schist, the remainder of limestone. The biggest of these lakes is Loch Corrib which separates Connemara and Iar Connacht from the central plain of Ireland. By the standards of western Europe Loch Corrib is large; it measures 45 kilometres in length and 21 kilometres at it's widest point, it's area of nearly 180 square kilometres is exceeded in Ireland only by Loch Neagh while no lake is of greater size in Britain, or lowland western Europe outside Scandinavia.

Rocks and regions of the Corrib basin.

The Corrib is a composite lake which comprises four different areas. The northwestern arm is a typical glacial lake, narrow, deep and with high hills on either side. At Doorus point (09E-49N) the lake expands into a large triangular basin, with hills to the north and west but fringed on the east by flat expanses of grey fretted limestone. Although this basin exceeds 30m in depth, islands are numerous; many are partially drowned drumlins, or small hillocks of glacial drift. Other drumlins, now completely submerged, form unexpected shoals and shallows. The middle lake is a long and irregular channel full of islands and reefs of limestone with many bordering inlets. The largest, Ballinduff Bay (29E-40N), is fed by limey springs, the large amounts of soft calcareous marl on the bottom are easily seen through it's clear water. The southern basin lies on limestone and is surrounded by bare rock, fens, raised bog and occasional stretches of agricultural land. Islands are few, even though this is the shallowest part of the lake with an average depth of only 2-3 metres.

The limestone lake

In the lower half of the lake, the only vertical element in the landscape is the wood and scrub which covers many of the shores and islands. Away from the shore all is flat, the wide surface of the lake, the great bog around the Clare river (31E-33N), the distant horizon broken only by the small hill of Knockma which lies ten miles to the east of the Corrib. The jagged complexity of eroding limestone beds is a recurring motif in the lakeside scenery. Along the shore, the rock is weathered into a pattern of hollows and pinnacles, so sharp as to prohibit barefoot exploration. Below the water surface decaying rock forms rugged and uneven reefs, a perpetual danger to passing boats. The many archipelagoes appear to be the remnants of nearly vanished horizontal strata, their ancient marine origin recorded from the Corrib woods include Toothwort, Bird's Nest Orchid (*Neottia nidus-avis*), Yellow Bird's Nest (*Monotropa hypopitys*) and Wood millet grass (*Milium effusum*), suggesting some continuity with ancient forest. A hundred years ago three metre high stumps of ancient yew trees (*Taxus baccata*) were rooted in the limestone pavement of Kylemore (19E-39N). It has been suggested that these were the last evidence of a mediaeval yew wood; it's memory survives in the name Aughnanure (the field of the yew trees). However these stumps seem to have since decayed.

A lovely wood of Oak, Ash and occasional Elm (*Ulmus montana*) is found at Kildermot (27E-38N) near Annaghdown, it grows on almost bare limestone. On the Hill of Doon a very different wood occurs, growing on ancient schist. This wood is similar to many Atlantic oak woods with abundant mosses, lichens and epiphytic ferns. Oak woods with Yew and Aspen (*Populus tremula*) grow on several islands east of Oughterard, and these have probably always been too small and too remote to merit more than occasional interference. In 1802 the botanist Walter Wade found oaks growing on Bilberry Island (14E-46N) and Wilde states this is an ancient woodland. Other islands were only created 150 years ago when the lake level was lowered. These are gradually developing a woodland cover, mainly Willow, Alder and Ash and this natural development is of great ecological interest.

BOTANICAL EXCURSIONS

There are many sites of botanical interest along the Corrib. In the north east Shrubby Cinquefoil, otherwise confined to the Burren in Co. Clare grows on the north west shore of Inchiquin (17E-46N), and in Ballynalty Bay(19E-51N). The Irish Lady's Tresses grows on the shore between Oughterard and Cornamona. The bogs and glacial hillocks and limestone pavement west of Knockferry (22E-40N) have a fully developed Burren flora, including Bearberry (*Arctostaphylos uva-ursi*), Juniper, Gentians, Mountain Avens (*Dryas octopetala*), Dark Red Helleborine (*Epipactis atrorubens*), as well Sundews and the rare Wood Bitter Vetch (*Vicia orobus*) which also occurs on several of the islands. A similar flora occurs around Luimnagh and Menlough (30E-29N), on the eastern shore. In the south east quarter Carrowbrowne raised bog (31E-34N) adjoins the lake and in a few places a full transition from open water through marsh and fen to bog remains despite turf cutting.

The flora of the north west arm is different and resembles that of Connemara. The magnificent St Dabeoc's Heath is common here as are Patrick's Cabbage and, in the water, the American Pipewort (*Eriocaulon aquaticum*).

SUMMER AND WINTER BIRDS

On every summer boat trip ducks, grebes, terns or gulls are certain to be seen, either close up or as distant silhouettes. The ornithology of the Corrib basin was studied for many years by Dr Tony Whilde. His reports provide detailed information on the birdlife of Loch Corrib. In summer, colonies of Arctic and Common Terns (*Sterna paradisea* and *S. hirundo*) are to be found on several of the rocky islands. Colonies of Gulls (*Larus canus, L.ridibundus, L.fuscus* and *L. marinus*) have so monopolized some islands that the former vegetation of trees and shrubs has been replaced by mixtures of weeds and bare rock. That such maritime birds should be found on freshwater is perhaps surprising but the equally maritime Cormorant (*Phalacrocorax carbo*) is also commonly seen. Other water birds which are

Pit and Pinnacle Weathering in Lakeshore Limestone

revealed by protruding fossil corals and shells. In many cases all that remains of a former limestone terrace is a gravel bank of chert, a harder black rock once embedded in the limestone. These islands have an irregular shoreline with offshore rocks and narrow promontories running far into the lake. In many places the limestone is porous and rivers flow underground, through caves and tunnels. At Cong all the water from Loch Mask filters through the limestone and the area is riddled with caverns and potholes. The Pigeon Hole and Kelly's Cave are amongst the most accessible and spectacular. Further west, near Ballymaglancy (11E-55N) more caves and swallow holes occur.

Further north, the limestone is replaced by older rocks; sandstone, granite, shale and slate. Here the lake is deeper, a trough gouged out by glaciers. Shorelines are of cobbles, or rounded rocks. The wooded islands are spaced out like a well ordered fleet of battleships. Shoals are rare and well marked. West of the lake the hills of Iar Connacht, which lie several miles inland south of Oughterard, now run down to the shore. Beyond Doon, these hills finally engulf the last arm of the lake where the quartzite of Lackavrea mountain overlooks the lonely island fortress of Hen's Castle. Five kilometres further west the lake ends at Maum Bridge and one is surrounded by the high corrie pitted hills and blanket bog of Connemara.

NAMES AND PEOPLE

The place names of the Corrib country take us far back into the region's history. It's present name is derived from Loch nOirbsen- the lake of Oirbsiu. Oiribsiu was an ancestor of the Conmhaicne, a reputedly Celtic people who settled by the lake. He is better known as Manannán mac Lir, the sea God whose memory is also preserved in the name of the Isle of Man. Loch Corrib 's scenic beauty is less well known than that of it's neighbours; the Burren and Connemara. In part, this is because it is less accessible; it must be explored by boat rather than by car. But less has been written about the lake. However two men have done much to remedy this deficit. William Wilde -the father of Oscar- wrote the 19th century account *Loch Corrib*. His house, called Moytura House, still stands today (17E-54N). In the 20th century, the late Dr Tony Whilde, who founded the Corrib Conservation Centre, greatly increased our knowledge of the area's natural history.

Entrance of Court Tomb, North of Aghalahard (13E-57N)

date the only evidence of these people's presence are some archaeological finds at the mouth of the river at Oughterard. At that time, the Corrib basin was a mosaic of forest, Pine in the northwest and Elm and Oak on the limestone interspersed with large swamps and fens extending far beyond their present limits. Today none of these forests remain.

The forests persisted undisturbed however, for at least a millennium until the first farmers appeared. The thin limestone soils that surround much of the Corrib were attractive to the early farmers of prehistoric times, both for their fertility and a lighter timber cover which was easier to clear than the timber on deeper heavier soils. These people have left their traces in the form of stone monuments and occasional archaeological finds. Hidden away amongst the fields and lanes are a number of ancient megalithic tombs, the last remnants of cultures so long vanished that we know little or nothing about their language, dress or politics. At Killimor (13E-57N), north of Cong, a well preserved court tomb stands in a recently cleared limestone pasture, poignantly linking the world of the first farmers to their most recent successors. East of Annaghkeen (21E-55N) the broken remnants of a court tomb are in a roadside field. At Annaghkeen (20E-55N) a stone enclosure hides a well preserved bronze age cist with it's surrounding cairn still intact. Other cairns are nearby.

Stone Circle North of Cong (16E-56N)

The presence of two huge stone cairns on the skyline, which overlook the entire region draw the traveller's thoughts back to this remote time. To the east, the cairn of Knockmaa (off the map) rises out of the plain some ten miles from the lake, while in the northwest the cairn of Seefin (05E-47N) crowns the hill which rises up from the lakeshore. In folk tradition Knockmaa was the dwelling place of Finnbheara, the king of the fairies of Connacht, while Seefin to the west was supposedly the seat of Fionn Mac Chumhaill. Almost certainly these kings and heroes are in reality pre-Christian deities whose cult may reach back to the Early Bronze Age when it is assumed that these cairns were constructed.

Several large burial cairns can also be seen on lower ground, Ballymagibbon cairn (18E-55N) is the most striking example of a large group of prehistoric monuments in the Cong area. Also in this district are standing stones, stone circles and a large enclosure (15E-56N) which may have had ceremonial purposes. This cluster probably dates to the Early Bronze Age (2,300-1,500 BC). A visitor to the stone circle at Tonaleeaun (16E-56N) can combine archaeology with botany, the stones enclosed by trees stand amongst a carpet of Wild Chives (*Allium schoenoprasum*).

PREHISTORIC LANDSCAPE CHANGE

By the Bronze Age a large part of the original forest cover on the limestone may have been felled; however abandoned fields would also have reverted to Hazel scrub and even Ash wood. In several places much of the limestone is now bare Burren-like karst (22E-50N), (19E-40N). Some areas of thin or even no soil show signs of former farming in the shape of dilapidated stone walls. Curiously, an unusual flora with plants of heathland and species typical of the Burren, such as Gentian and Juniper grow on this ground. Were these areas once ancient fertile fields? Several millennia later, 19th century observers noted that farmers still burnt the grass and sod of fields as a method of soil enrichment. This practice if repeated too often would allow rain to wash away the always thin and stoney soil, leaving only the bare rock. The bare limestone rock would then be suitable for colonization by it's present distinctive flora.

Less is known about the prehistoric people and vegetation around the north west arm of the lake. Today much of the area is covered by blanket bog but in Connemara this bog only developed on the hillsides from 1000 BC onwards; before that the poor quartzite soils probably carried a covering of pine forest. The decline of this forest type, now vanished from Ireland, is linked to repeated burning of the ground probably by early pastoralists. The visitor to Hen's Castle (99E-50N) should complete the trip by rowing across to the cliff from which Lackavrea mountain rises; here fragments of Oak and Birch wood still linger in an area otherwise covered by grass and bog.

By 1000 BC the raised bog of Carrowbrowne would have been well established and gradually encroaching on the surrounding fens and open water. Geological survey maps show that much of this bog is underlain by shells and clay, typical lake bottom deposits.

HILL FORTS, CAISEALS
AND ANCIENT KINGDOMS

In the centuries before the birth of Christ, iron working became established in Ireland, One great monument dates from this period. An enclosure known as An Cathair Mhór (25E-51N) crowns a hill north of Headford. It is much too large to be a simple homestead and is thought to be a hill

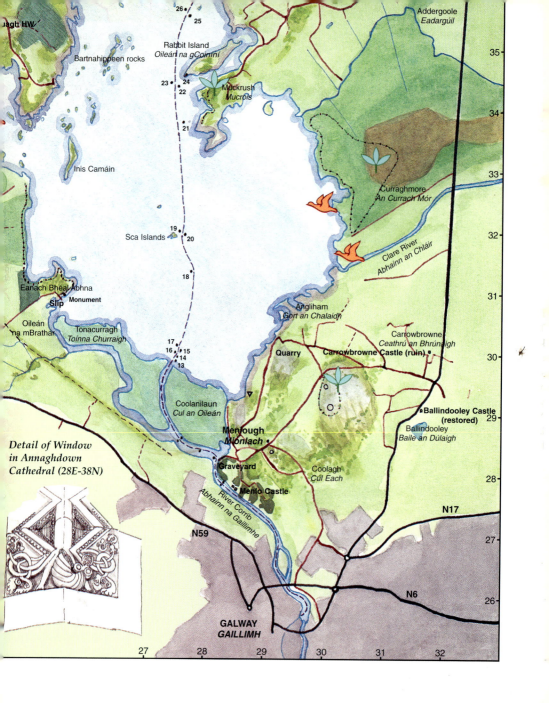

Purple Loosestrife *Northern Bedstraw* *Bird's Foot*

Marsh Helleborine *Meadow Thistle*

Marsh Orchid

PLANTS OF THE SHORE

The rocky shore line of the lake -including islands- probably exceeds 100 kilometres. A distinctive assembly of plants grows there. Some are large and colourful such as Wild Angelica *(Angelica sylvestris)*, Purple Loosestrife *(Lythrum salicaria)* or Hemp Agrimony *(Eupatorium cannabinum)*. Others, although smaller, are equally colourful such as the lilac tinted Water Mint *(Mentha aquatica)* or the yellow Lesser Spearwort *(Ranunculus flammula)*. Some species such as the Northern Bedstraw *(Galium boreale)* have a very local distribution in Ireland which is largely confined to limestone lake shores and a few mountain ledges, others like the Bird's Foot *(Lotus corniculatus)* occur widely in grassland.

PLANTS OF FENLAND

Much of the low lying ground around the Corrib floods every winter and supports a dense vegetation of the sedge known as Black Bog Rush *(Schoenus nigricans)*. In itself rather drab, this vegetation is the habitat of some striking flowers including species of Marsh Orchid *(Dactylorhiza sp.)*. While the taxonomy of these plants is complex, all have heavy spikes of pink or purple flowers which are best seen in June and July. The Meadow Thistle *(Cirsium dissectum)* is very abundant on wet lake shores and islands where it grows along side Black Bog Rush. It's purple flower heads are seen in July. The Marsh Helleborine orchid *(Epipactis palustris)*, occurs in calcareous wetlands throughout Europe but has a patchy distribution as wetlands have been greatly reduced in extent . It occurs in great profusion in some of the marshes around the Corrib.

The English conquest

The Elizabethan and Cromwellian wars brought ruin to all the old ecclesiastical centres around the lake. Most tower houses and castles were wrecked or abandoned and the Gaelic law and culture of both Norman and Irish suppressed. In addition the remaining old woodlands were all but eradicated .

A side effect of this destruction was that many of the former merchant families of Galway, the Lynches, Blakes, Bodkins, Martins, D'Arcys and Skerrets retreated to the countryside and acquired estates around the Corrib. In an abandoned orchard at Ballinduff (30E-41N) an 18th century inscription on a garden gateway commemorates John Skerret and Lucy Lockey. In the woods at Clydagh (21E-43N), an inscription from 1670 commemorates Elizabeth Staunton. As recently as 1910, Blakes still lived

Menlough Castle (28E-27N)

Ruined Castle and 18th Century Walled Garden at Ballinduff (30E-41N)

at Menlough Castle (28E-27N). In many of the lakeside churchyards, tombs of these families still remain. Some appear incongruous, as the D'Arcy memorial urn in the little enclosure at Billypark (18E-42N), others are unexpected such as the tomb in Killanin Churchyard (18E-37N) of Major Poppleton, husband of one of the Martins of Ross and Napoleon's guard on St Helena. Mansions such as Clydagh House or the more recent Ashford Castle (14E-54N) still look out over the lake, but many more are now roofless and decayed. In places such as Annaghkeen or Ballycurrin (19E-49N), abandoned castles flank the remnants of 18th century big houses. While many houses have gone, often woodlands planted at this time still survive, for example around Cong, Clydagh, and Menlough. These are easily recognised by the presence of Cherry laurel, Beech, and Box.

Memorial Urn at Billypark (18E-42N)

THE 19TH CENTURY SCENE

19th century engravings and reports show that most of the countryside was bare of trees and Hazel scrub. Islands now heavily timbered such as Illaunaneel (27E-38N), were then divided into fields, and the old walls still run through the modern wood. Settlement was characterised by clusters of thatched cottages called Clachans. Many of these still survive especially in the country around Headford where mixed groups of thatched cottages and modern bungalows are found. Tillage and especially potato cultivation was far more widespread, old cultivation ridges are visible on several of the larger islands. Conversely many of the stoney limestone tracts, now intensively farmed were of little use other than for rough grazing. Large empty areas of heath occurred on both sides of the lake at Cloghmoyne (22E-49N), Luimnagh, Annagdown, Cong and Callownamuck (22E-40N).

Contemporary travellers report a relatively prosperous people around Headford and Cong, but in Connemara life was still simple, even poverty stricken. The larger islands were inhabited and traffic on the lake was greater then than now. At least fifty single masted

	Limestone Bedrock
	Slates or Sandstone Bedrock
	Schist, Quartzite or Granite Bedrock
	Limestone Pavement
	Raised Bog
	Blanket Bog
	Fen, Rough Grazing and Other Non Agricultural Land
	Rocky Limestone Shore
	Old Woodland (including Oak, Elm, Ash)
	Scrub and Wood on previously cleared land (including Hazel, Ash, Willow)
	Planted Broad leafed Woodland (including Beech, Larch, Ash)
	Conifer Plantation (including Sitka Spruce and Lodgepole Pine)
O	Well Preserved Dún or Ringfort
O	Badly Preserved Dún or Ringfort
▽	Megalithic Tombs and Cists
✳	Cairn
+	Cillín (Children's Burial Ground)
⊕	Cillín in enclosure
HW	Holy Well
	Main Road
	Other Surfaced Roads
- - - -	Unsurfaced Roads and Tracks
	Marked Walker's Path
	Unmarked Walks
	Navigation Channel
•137	Numbered Beacon or Post
	Area of Botanical Interest
	Good Birdwatching Site

Tracks, footpaths and unstructured walks shown on this map are not necessarily rights of way. Walkers should appreciate that when they walk over any property, that they do so entirely at their own risk.

Navigation Channel
The Numbered Posts or Beacons are those of the Corrib Navigation Trust. Information on the navigation channel courtesy of Lough Corrib Navigation Trustees.

How to locate sites
The co-ordinates used on this map are those of the National Grid. The first figure of a reference is the Easting co-ordinate which is read from West to East; the second is the Northing co-ordinate which is read from South to North. The location sought will lie in the square East/North of the co-ordinates.
Example: Annaghkean Castle (20E-44N)

Acknowledgements; We would like to thank Mr Mícheál Keaney, Gordon D'Arcy and Paul Gosling for their help and encouragement.

Based on the Ordnance Survey by permission of the Government (Permit No. 6644)
Published in 1998 by TÍR EOLAS, Newtownlynch, Kinvara, Co Galway.
©Text Cilian Roden
©Artwork Anne Korff
ISBN 1 873821 08 5
Printed in Ireland by BETAPRINT, Dublin.

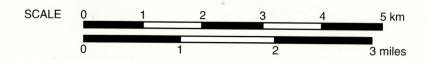

BIRDS OF THE LAKE

There is a wide variety of shore and water birds to be seen on Loch Corrib. This variety reflects the different habitats of the lake ranging from deep, exposed open water to sheltered and shallow reed beds. In summer large flocks are seen less often than small groups. In winter however, very large concentrations of Coot *(Fulica atra)* are known to occur in the lower lake. In the past equally large numbers of wintering Pochard *(Aythya ferina)* were recorded but, more recently, numbers have declined. Conversely the Common Scoter *(Melanitta nigra)* is a recent arrival that now nests in very small numbers on Loch Corrib - one of a handful of lakes in Ireland where it is found. Two of the most frequently seen ducks are the Tufted Duck *(Aythya fuligula)* and the Merganser *(Mergus serrator)*. Both breed on the lake and can be seen far from shore. The Whitefronted Goose *(Anser albifrons flavirostris)*, is a winter visitor which feeds near the raised bog and callows at Curraghmore (30E-32N), where up to 80 may be seen. At least ten pairs of the Great Crested Grebe *(Podiceps cristatus)* nest around the lake they are most attractive birds in summer plumage and their courting display is a fascinating spectacle, if one is lucky enough to see it.

There are many islands on the lake and all have an atmosphere of calm and detachment from the mainland. The following are amongst the most interesting;

Inchagoill has both early Christian remains, a small sandy beach, and a long woodland walk. It is planned to remove the existing commercial conifers and replace them with Scots Pine and deciduous trees in the near future.

The island fortress of Hen's Castle is a good example of an early stone Castle.

The islands off Oughterard; Bilberry, Bronteen, Coad and Urkaunmore have Oak and Aspen woods which appear to be very old and for naturalists are well worth visiting.

In the south of the lake several groups of limestone islands and reefs are home to both interesting plants and birds. The Barnahippeen Rocks are both interesting and seldom visited.

The mainland shores obviously do not require boats: walking boots, bicycles and cars are the needed equipment. By car it is possible to circumnavigate the whole lake in about four hours without halting, but such a journey will serve little purpose. Much better to drive to a selected spot and walk the shoreline. Many of the shores of the Corrib are open to pedestrians. The bogland of the southeast and the mountain slopes of the northwest arm are hard going but their loneliness is an attraction. The limestone shores are easier to traverse and most attractive for those who appreciate wildflowers. Areas worth exploring on foot include the caves, woods and prehistoric monuments around Cong; the limestone pavement and glacial hillocks south of Carrowmoreknock which contain a flora which rivals that of the Burren, The Western Way from Maum to Oughterard is a marked footpath with striking mountain and lake scenery. Between the Clare and Cregg rivers lies a complex of fen and raised bog with wintering Greenland Geese. An expedition to the cairn on Seefin mountain will combine archaeology with an all encompassing view of the Lake.

Bicycles are an excellent way to explore the lanes that run down to the lake and to visit many of the more secluded historical monuments. There are many pleasant pubs along the lake which should not be passed by for example at Maum Bridge, Cornamona, Cong, Greenfields, Kilbeg, Tullokyne, Oughterard and Clonbur.

Books

The classic book on Loch Corrib was written over a century ago in 1867 by William Wilde, simply titled *Loch Corrib*. It has been reprinted on several occasions this century. *The Corrib Country* by Richard Hayward was published in 1943; both are out of print at present. More recently, Maurice Semple has privately published several books about Galway and the Corrib. These can still be bought in Galway city. For naturalists, the Corrib Conservation centre, Ardsallagh, Oughterard, published a series of booklets on Corrib natural history, these can also be bought in Galway Book shops.

PRICE £5.95

ISBN 1-873821-08-5